My Money Cheat Sheet – The Pillars of Personal Finance: Vol. 1: Credit, Taxes and Budgeting

by

Sam Woke

My Money Cheat Sheet – The Pillars of Personal Finance: Vol. 1: Credit, Taxes and Budgeting

Published in the United States of America.

1.   Business & Money / Finance
2.   Business & Money / Personal Finance / Budgeting & Money Management

ISBN-10: 1793117411
ISBN-13: 978-1793117410

Dedication

I dedicate this book to all the students out there that want to be ready for the real world, and a very real way. The ones that know that, the only way to guarantee success, is to put in the work; and that knowledge is power.

Honor And Appreciation

Leah Coicou

I am so grateful for your love, and your light in my life. I would not have been able to pursue this book without your confidence in me, and your unwavering support. I love you to the moon and back, my beautiful, ever-supporting wife.

WORKBOOK

Grab a copy of the workbook!

Do you have the memory capacity of a goldfish? Follow along in the workbook! It has useful content to help you remember and apply these golden nuggets of knowledge to your life.

Get A Copy on Amazon now for free!

Table of Contents

INTRODUCTION 1

Chapter 1: Budgeting Like a Boss 3

Overview: Paying yourself first 4

Paying Yourself Last 5

Real savings vs. fake savings................................13

The 50/30/20 rule 14

Chapter 2: Credit Cards and Credit Scores 16

The Credit Bureaus 18

What Affects Your Credit?......................................18

Starting Sooner Is Better..21

Interest Rates (aka APR)..24

How is interest calculated? 26

What is a Credit Score (or Credit Rating)? 30

Chapter 3: Credit Score Factors................................33

The Factors 33

1.   Payment History 33

My story..34

2. Credit Utilization ratio 38

3. Length of Credit History 42

4. New Credit and Credit Inquiries 44

5. Number of credit account types 46

My story, continued 46

Chapter 4: Applying for a Credit Card 50

Secured Credit card (New/Bad credit) 50

Pros 51

Cons 52

Chapter 5: Tips and 55

Suggestions 55

Creditors = High School Girls 56

Tracking Your Credit 57

Set It and Forget It 58

Become an authorized user 59

Making credit card payments 60

Chapter 6: Credit Card Debt 63

Strategies for Paying off Debt 64

Other options 69

How to deal with the stress of debt........................71

Defaulting (Hardships) 74

    1.   Pay off the balance..............................74

    2.   Negotiate to pay less 75

    3.   File bankruptcy 76

    (CONSULT AN EXPERT) 76

    4.   Do nothing. 76

My story, continued…..80

Chapter 7: Taxes 84

Quick definitions...85

What is a tax exemption/allowance?....................86

Summary of exemptions (subject to change) 87

    Single with no kids.......................................88

    Married with no kids (Filing jointly)................89

    Married with one or more kids 89

When should you update your W4/W9?...............91

The W-2 (employee)...91

The 1099 (Independent contractor)......................92

My story continued…..92

Deductions 96

Standard Deduction vs Itemizing Deductions.......96

Other questions & answers about taxes................105

Conclusion...108

Don't let this distract you from the fact... 109

One. More. Thing. 109

References...110

About the author 115

INTRODUCTION

While it's great that schools teach us everything from complicated mathematical theorems and underwater basket weaving, our educational system could still lacks in one major category: personal finance. The reality is, most high school and college curriculums lack in personal finance courses for whatever reason. This book poses as a guide to students survive in today's America. This series will be useful, relatable, and actionable. The hope is to help those who are lacking in the area of personal finance. We'll cover hot topics in an easy, methodical way—with full-fledged, non-scary, step by step mathematical instructions. So easy, that no one will be left behind.

Nobody's telling you to read this whole book in one sitting, but it's so short you just might. But hey, this stuff, no matter how boring it sounds, is very important. It is the difference between financial stability, versus struggling with debt your whole life.

Once you stop and realize that everything you do, from here on out will drastically affect your life, you tend to be a bit more careful and intentional with your financial decisions. Financial knowledge is key, and with it, you'll start building good habits that will shape your life for the better.

DISCLAIMER: This book and the content provided herein are simply for educational purposes and do not take the place of legal advice from a financial advisor. Every effort has been made to ensure that the content provided in this book is accurate and helpful for readers at publishing time. However, this is not an exhaustive treatment of the subjects. No liability is assumed for losses or damages due to the information provided. You are responsible for your own choices, actions, and results. You should consult a financial advisor for your specific needs.

Chapter 1: Budgeting Like a Boss

First, we're covering the grandfather of finance, budgeting.

Budgeting is the equivalent of warming up in band class, or getting an oil change. It feels like a waste of time and can be super annoying, but in the end, you're better for it. In this chapter, you're going to learn about how to get your money going in the right direction. Most of the time, the solution isn't always about making more money. It's about managing your money correctly so that you can have a fun, balanced life no matter how much you make.

Some people don't want to take the time to make a budget or set up a good direct deposit strategy, and because of that, they never know why they don't have as much money as they thought. Money disappears at the blink of an eye if we don't give it somewhere to go. The worst feeling is thinking you had $150 in your checking account, and see -$3.23 when you check your balance. Yikes.

Overview: Paying yourself first

The biggest thing to learn is **paying yourself first**. It means to put a certain amount of money aside as soon as you get paid that you don't touch. That money will be reserved specifically for savings or investing. This money is taken out of your paycheck even before paying your bills, or buying groceries. If you don't make plans to "pay yourself first" you will spend money you were planning to save. In my case, that money was always spent on gadgets from Amazon lol… The easiest way to do this is to have part of your check direct deposited into your savings account, and the rest into your checking account.

As boring as it sounds, we need to be intentional about saving. It may be tough to have less money to spend at first, but you'll learn to live below your means. That's one of the first ways to rise above "living paycheck to paycheck". And dude, when you need that money, you'll thank God you had it.

Paying Yourself Last

Some people just save whatever is left in their account at the end of the month. This is called **paying yourself last**. The problem with that is, you never know how much you'll spend that month if you don't give yourself a limit. It's not that you don't think saving money is important, it's that you aren't making saving a certain amount of money important. Paying yourself first should be as important as paying rent. The closer you get to that mindset, the easier it will be to execute.

PRO TIP

Budget "personal fun money". This is money that you set aside for yourself every check. Those funds are for you to do whatever the heck you want without any guilt! If you add this to your budget, you will learn to live below your means, and let your budget do its thing. You can even have this money direct deposited into another account all together.

Anyway, this is what it looks like if you pay yourself last.

Step 1) Money is direct deposited into checking account.

Step 2) Pay bills.

Step 3) Spend money on monthly expenses.

Step 4) Whatever is leftover is transferred to your savings account.

But The "Pay Yourself First" System is:

Step 1) Set it up with payroll so a predetermined amount of money you want to save is direct deposited into your savings account, and the rest goes into your checking account.

Step 2) You use auto-pay in your checking account to pay your bills and expenses. (Your savings account isn't touched)

Step 3) If you really need more money for expenses, transfer money from your savings to checking.

Once it's set up, you'll be able to map out saving for things in the future because your savings will grow at a constant rate without fail. For example: If you save $200/mo you know for a fact you'll have $1,000 in 5 months. If you keep dipping into your savings account for monthly expenses, it could mean two things: you need to take control of your spending habits, or you need to adjust the amount sent to your checking account accordingly. It's all about finding the right balance and sticking to it. The first step is knowing how much you can save from every check. And to do that you would need to have a budget that tells you: 1) how much your bills are, 2) how much your expenses usually are, and 3) how much "personal fun money" you want from every check.

Below we're going to learn how you can create a budget specific to you when the time comes. You can use Microsoft excel or even good old pencil and paper. There's also a table already set up in the workbook #LazyLife.

Emergency Savings

The first thing you need to do is build an emergency savings fund as fast as you can. (At least 3 months of expenses saved up). You will learn how much you can save from each check by creating a budget.

Creating A Budget

Step 1: Calculate your average net balance.

Look at your bank statements and fill in all fields of the table below that apply to you. The more months you include, the more accurate the calculation. Get it all in there. Netflix, the gym, or your monthly subscription for beard oil. Total each category in the grey boxes. (Note: If you have annual fees and memberships, bring them to the monthly equivalent by dividing the amount by 12)

Monthly Income	
Income	
Job 1:	$
Job 2:	$
Job 3:	$
Passive Income	$

Monthly Expense			Monthly Expense	
Housing	$		*Miscellaneous*	$
Rent/Mortgage 1:	$		Student Loans	$
Rent/Mortgage 2:	$		Groceries	$
HOA fees	$		Gym Membership	$
Lawn/Pool/Snow maintenance	$		Subscription 1:	$
Auto/ Commute	$		Subscription 2:	$
Auto Payment 1:	$		*Donations*	$
Auto Payment 2:	$		Tithe	$
Gas	$		Other	$
Public Transit	$		Other	$
Taxi/Uber/Lyft	$		*Savings*	$
Parking	$		Retirement/ 401K	$
Insurance	$		Emergency	$
Renters/Home owners	$		Investing	$
Car	$		Other:	$
Health	$		Other:	$
Utilities	$		*Fun Money*	$
Electric	$		Eating out	$
Gas	$		Travel/Activates	$
Water	$		Shopping	$
Entertainment	$		*Other*	$
Cable	$			$
Internet	$			$
Phone	$			$
Streaming Service 1:	$			$
Streaming Service 2:	$			$

Net	
Total Income	$
- Total Expenses	$
= Net Balance	$

Step 2: Analyze your situation

Is your net balance positive or negative? Is it negative, or a lower than you thought it should? Why is that? Find out what the issue is. Look at the categories, what have you been spending your money on? Is it something stupid? Something wasteful? Maybe it's time make a change? The next step is to build an emergency fund, but if you keep spending all your extra money, than you'll never be able to do it. You two options are either to spend less, or make more money.

If you're net balance is a positive number, congrats! You have space to save money! Move on to step 3.

Step 3: Building Emergency Fund

After you calculate how much extra money you have left over every month, build your emergency fund ASAP using that amount. Emergency funds are your buffer against the pitfalls of life. Somethings always coming, if it's not here, it's on it's way. Your car's radiator gives, your glasses fall and break while on the treadmill. It happens; it's a part of life.

Your emergency fund should 3 months of your monthly expenses saved. This provides a good buffer for unplanned require expenses, or if you're in-between jobs. You sleep better at night knowing you got some cash saved up.

Step 4: Setting Up Your Budget

1. Now that your emergency fund is intact, it's time to really create your budget. First thing you need to do is subtract your income by your expenses. You've already done this.

2. Next, subtract out, how much money you want to save.

3. Next, subtract out, how much you want for fun money. This needs to be done last.

4. Now you can set up a more specific direct deposit situation. If you go to your payroll administrator, you can have them deposit different portions of your paycheck into different accounts automatically. No chance of spending that money, if it never goes in that other account in the first place.

5. **Account #1**: **Checking account for bills and expenses:** Everything outside of money you you're going to generally save, or save for fun money goes in here.

   Account #2: **Savings account**. Decided what the amount is and have is direct deposited in here automatically.

   Account #3: **Fun money**. To be use for anything you want.

Example

Mike makes $400 a week, his rent is $600/month, and his other bills and expenses are $400/month. So that means monthly he makes about $1,600 and spends $1,000, and has a remainder is $600/month. But somehow he never seems to be able to save every month. After doing the math on his cash flow, and seeing he has $600 left every month, he decides to open another account and direct deposit $400 automatically. He learns to live off of $200/month of fun money, and after 6 months, he has over $2,400 in his savings account.

Real savings vs. fake savings

Know the difference between real savings, and a discount disguised as savings. Real savings is when you find a way to lower your recurring monthly expenses in an effort to have a bigger remaining balance. Fake savings are actually a discount. It's a one-time reduced price of an item or service.

People don't realize there's a difference, and that is one of the reasons why some never seem to be able to save money. Perfect example is when you go to a Black Friday sale and get a sweet new flat screen for $400 when it's usually $1000. You saved $600 on the TV's price but it won't really improve your monthly savings. All it did was increase your monthly expenses.

An example of real savings is if you finally paid off your car note (Gucci!) and now you have an extra $350/month. That's real savings! Now that doesn't mean you should spend $350 more a month, instead save or invest it. For example, if you really want to stay ahead of the game, maybe increase the direct deposit to your savings by $350 and live your life at the same pace.

Examples of REAL savings

- Paying off car or student loans
- Using coupons to save on groceries monthly
- Finding cheaper car or home insurance
- Consolidating your loans to a lower interest rate
- Refinancing your home to a lower interest rate

The 50/30/20 rule

A great rule of thumb to start off is the 50/30/20 rule. Of course, this method may not work for everyone but it's a wonderful way to get you on the right path with your budget.

- 50% of your income after taxes should take care of living expenses, such as your mortgage, groceries, gas and utilities
- 30% should go to things like eating out, entertainment, and clothes. Fun money!
- 20% should go towards long term things like paying off debt faster, emergency saving account, 401k, benefits, and investing

That sums up budgeting. Though it's seems time-consuming and boring it's the foundation of all finance. Next we'll go through the gateway drug of debt, credit cards.

Chapter 2: Credit Cards and Credit Scores

In the real world, young adults are immediately flooded with credit card offers on their eighteenth birthday, or when they're headed off to college. To many people, 'credit card' implies two things: shopping and debt, but they imply so much more than that. Credit cards are a huge part of our lives. As you leave home, or begin making your own finance decisions, you'll realize both the value and danger of credit cards.

Just so everyone's on the same page.

- Your "credit" (or credit history) is basically your financial record when you borrow money
- Your credit report is a document illustrating your credit history. Much like your transcripts
- Your credit score is a numerical value that rates your credit report. Like your GPA

Credit cards are used for big and small reasons such as reservations, reward points, car repairs, medical bills, and emergencies. The most important thing to understand about credit cards is that they are **a tool to build your credit**. Credit is all about building trust with financial institutions and creditors. You've heard of street cred in the hood, well this is street cred of adulthood.

You graduated college, and got a wonderful job so now you can be totally financially independent. Probably not. Just because you have a nice job doesn't mean you're financially set. You need to build credit, and habits that will keep you safe from debt. Do you think the credit card companies have your best interest at heart? Do they expect us to get it right immediately out of high school or college? Let me fill you in, **NOPE**

With credit cards, you are borrowing money that you promise to repay in the future. As you continue to use your credit card, and pay it back monthly, it builds your credit score and the trust of banks, and other institutions. So, if you don't make your payments, you are hurting your credit. On the flipside, if you make on-time payments and hit the other factors — explained later — you'll be on the path to the promise land.

The Credit Bureaus

Credit Bureaus (CBs) are institutions dedicated to tracking credit information of individuals and businesses. The three major national credit bureaus are Experian, Equifax and TransUnion. They track your credit history and put it in your credit report. That report is also where you find your credit score.

What Affects Your Credit?

While credit cards are usually the beginning of our financial credit history. There's a misconception that if you make on-time payments on **any** recurring bill, you are building credit. NOPE! Fact is, not all bills affect your credit. Here's a list of bills that people think will increase their credit score and **do not** (but can hurt your credit):

- Rent
- Cell phone bill
- Utility bill
- Cable or Internet bill
- Gym membership
- Insurance payments
- Private loans (can hurt your credit but can't build your credit)

No matter how many times you pay your rent on-time, it will never help increase your credit score because those type of bills aren't affiliated with credit institutions. They can't help your credit score, but they can hurt it. If for whatever reason, you stop making payments, they will send you to collections or small claims court. This will show up on your credit report and negatively affect your credit score. If you miss payments do your best to pay them off ASAP. You can call your creditor to explain your situation, they may work with you, which buys you time and helps you build rapport. The higher the debt gets, the more likely they will send you to collections.

Here are the types of things that can increase your credit score:

- Mortgage payments
- Credit cards
- Auto loans
- Most Student loans
- Judgements and liens

Why is this important? It's simple. If you ever get into a pinch financially, and need to decide what to pay with the money you have, it makes financial sense to pay for the things that will affect your credit first. Those items could have a long-term effect on your financial future. So, we got it twisted! For some reason, we think it's okay to miss a credit card payment, but we'll never miss a phone bill! That's the exact opposite of what we should be doing. The credit card should be priority because missed payments could affect our credit. Paying all your bills on time is the best option, but sometimes the struggle is real!

One time, in college, I went crazy and bought a new pair of jeans, a school hoody, and shades for a basketball game when I didn't have the money in my checking account. All my friends were going to the game. They had their school swag so I wanted my own. Well, when the bill came, I had to choose between paying the credit card bill, my gym membership, or repaying a friend. I opted to pay for the gym and my friend. WRONG! My credit score dropped because of it. I should've paid my credit card and skipped the gym membership because missing my payment screwed me over!

Starting Sooner Is Better

Many young adults fear getting a credit card because the thought of being in debt terrifies them. Credit cards are tricky, and if you don't understand how they work you should not sign up for one. But yeah, that's why you're reading this book! So that you do understand them. The truth is, if you understand how they work, and are financially responsible, you are better off starting your credit sooner than later. Here are several reasons why:

1) **Bad credit is better than no credit**. In this world, you can still be approved for credit if you have bad credit. The caveat is that your interest rates will be very high, you'll have limited to no perks, and very harsh late payment fees. On the other hand, if you don't have a credit history at all, some creditors will reject your application without hesitation. Take it like this. If you're looking to buy something on Amazon, are you going to buy the product with thousands of reviews, or the one that looks nice but has zero reviews and ratings? To me products with no reviews don't even appear in my peripheral when I'm shopping online. It's like I have tunnel vision for only the products that have reviews. Naturally you don't trust products that don't have someone else's stamp of approval. Credit institutions are the same way. They shop for us as customers just as we shop for stuff on Amazon.

2) **Credit takes time to build**. If you start early, your credit will be in a better position when you need a loan. That time comes faster than you think. Don't wait until you have a baby on the way, and your car won't start, and your AC went out in the middle of a Texas summer, to work on your credit. Also "Length of credit history" is a factor in your credit score. (Explained later) Having a credit card that has been open for a long time helps to increase your credit score even if you don't use it a lot.

PRO TIP

DON'T USE OR OPEN ANY CREDIT CARDS IF YOU DON'T HAVE A JOB OR ACCESS TO MONEY! EVEN IF THEY PROMISE A MILLION FREE POINTS, AND A NEW CAR, AND FREE TACOS FOR LIFE! (Actually, I might take a chance on the tacos)

You shouldn't use your credit card when you don't have the money to pay it off. Your balance will increase and so will your interest. Then you'll get sent to collections. It's a stupid idea to use your credit card for something of luxury, instead of necessity when you know darn well the bill is coming next month, and you won't be able to pay it. What? Did you think they would've let you slide a few months? No way. Never. If it's not a necessity, or an emergency, do not charge anything on your credit card, and put yourself in that situation. Take it out of your wallet, ask buddies to spot you, ask your parents for money, do anything but use your credit card if you're broke. We know that grandma loves you and thinks you're a little biscuit with a buttery flaky crust. But creditors don't! They will hold you accountable by reporting you to the CBs. STOP USING YOUR CARD.

Interest Rates (aka APR)

One of the major components of a credit card, and loans is the interest rate or APR (Annual Percentage Rate). Interest is the fee associated with borrowing money, and it's how creditors make their money. They lend you some money, then give you time to pay it back for a "small fee". Creditors are "banking" on the fact that you aren't going to pay your whole balance every month. When you don't, they smash you with an interest fee on top of your balance. But here's the secret: **If you don't want to pay interest, pay the entire balance every month**. What makes interest so scary is how fast it builds and multiplies. Albert Einstein said, "Compound Interest is the 8th wonder of the world", he's talking about investing your money, receiving interest payments, and reinvesting it. Your assets grow exponentially because the income you receive from investing begins to receive interest on itself! It's a beautiful thing and will be covered in a future book. But guess what? If you fall into debt, the same could happen to you but in reverse. If you are charged interest and you don't pay it off that month, next month, your interest will be assessed including the interest you accrued last month. And guess what? This is how most people fall in a deep bottomless pit of debt. Interest keeps accruing on top of itself. It's like an infection.

Effective interest rate. Never heard of it? They don't want you to. Effective interest rate is the true interest you pay during your loan. The APR is usually in big bold letters and clearly visible. But sometimes, that's not the whole story. Sometimes the APR is a certain amount for ONLY the first year and then it becomes something else after year one. Most of the time — if not all the time — it's a higher interest rate. So definitely, double check and triple check the terms and conditions for any hidden fees as well. Ask as many questions as you can to make sure you're getting what you think you're getting.

How is interest calculated?

Though it's called annual percentage rate, creditors calculate your interest **per day**, not per year. They charge interest per how many days you have a certain balance. Ever wonder how they come up with what to charge you for interest? Let's find out.

The Boring Math

Let's say in January you get a credit card with 20% APR. First you need to know how much interest you're charged per day. Interest per day is called **periodic interest rate (PIR).**

The way it's calculated is: **PIR** = 20% / 365 = 0.055%. (FYI: Some banks divide by 360 instead of 365)

Then you need to calculate your **average daily balance (ADB)**.

ADB = (Jan 1st balance / Number of days in the month) + (Jan 2nd balance / Number of days in the month) + etc... **NOTE**: If your balance stays the same for a certain number of days you can multiply that number of days by the balance total instead of doing that calculation for every day it's the same individually.

Formula (**PIR X ADB** X 31 days)

So, say you have a balance of $500 from January 1st to January 15th, the ADB up to that point would look like this:

ADB = ($500 X 15 days) / 31 days = $241.94 for Jan 1st to Jan 15th.

Let's say on the 16th you make a payment of $200, which brings your remaining balance to $300, then you don't make another payment in this month. Your **ADB** for that period would look like this:

ADB = ($300 X 16 days) / 31 days = $154.84 for Jan 16th - Jan 31st.

And so total **ADB** for January would be:

ADB = $241.94 + $154.84 = $369.78

The amount of interest that you will be charged and added to your account balance in February will be:

ADB X PIR X 31 days = $369.78 X 0.055% X 31 = $6.31

So, at the beginning of next month (February) your new balance will be the remaining balance in January plus the interest accrued from January, which is: $300 + $6.31 = $306.31.

That was a lot of math, but know this:

- The lower your credit score the higher your interest will be.
- The higher the interest rate, the more interest you will pay.
- The higher your balance on a credit card, the more interest you'll pay.
- But if your credit score is higher, you will be eligible for lower interest rates.

Always Look for Lower Rates

As your credit score increases you should constantly be on the lookout for lower interest rates. This includes credit cards and other loans such as: student loans, auto loans, and mortgages. From personal experience, after you make 6 or more on-time payments, or your credit score increases, you should contact the credit institution and request a lower interest rate. I've done this several times. Don't miss out on any opportunity to save money. Creditors aren't going to always tell you that you're eligible for lower rates, so that they can keep charging you the most interest possible. To them, it's business, so it's up to you to keep track.

FICO credit score

FICO stands for Fair Isaac Corporation. It was the first company to provide a credit score based on how risky a consumer is. The bulk of banks in the United States use FICO scores to decide if it will be risky to offer credit to potential borrowers, and at what interest rate.

What is a Credit Score (or Credit Rating)?

If your credit report is like your transcripts, a credit score is your GPA. The score tells lenders how much risk they have if they lend money to you. The higher your credit score the more favorable your interest rates will be. **Note**: There are many institutions that calculate credit scores in their own way and even change the numbers for the ranges as they see fit. (ex. Outstanding credit may be 740-850 for institution A and 800-850 for institution B)

The numbers below are consistent with the FICO credit score ranges. The scores are usually given a number between 300 and 850. Here is what they mean:

- 750 - 850: Outstanding Credit. You are considered very, very low credit risk by creditors and qualify for the best interest rates, pay terms and features

- 700 - 749: Very Good Credit. You are considered a low credit risk by creditors and would generally qualify for low interest rates, pay terms, and features.

- 680 - 699: Good Credit. You are considered moderate risk and will usually be approved for loans and cards with decent rates and terms.

- 620 - 679: Okay Credit. You are a higher than moderate credit risk, and you'll be approved for a good amount of loans and cards but not the best rates and terms.

- 550 - 619: Bad credit. You are considered high credit risk and you will have to shop around to find a creditor to even approve an application for you, and your rates and terms will not be favorable. Maybe consider a secure card. (Explained later)

- Below 550: Very bad credit. You are considered an extreme credit risk and will probably not be able to find someone willing to approve you for a loan or card. You may have to look at credit repair and may only qualify for a secured card, but even that may not be guaranteed. But for real though, don't give up. You just need the tools and education to turn it around. You've taken the first step in reading this book. *High Five.

Chapter 3: Credit Score Factors

I used to think if I just made the minimum monthly payment on-time, I would have a good credit score. Oh no baby, that's not the way it works. **Your credit score will never go from good to great unless you hit each and every one of these factors.**

The Factors

1. Payment History

Payment history (specifically on-time payment history) is the largest factor of your credit score and is worth 35% of it. Trust comes with reliability and consistency. If you don't pay on-time, why would they trust you. Sadly, in some cases if you miss even **one payment, your score could drop!** So, watch yourself.

Note: The CB counts factors in both recurring loans (i.e. credit cards) and installment loans (i.e. auto loans, mortgages, etc...).

PRO TIP

If you accidentally miss a payment, call immediately to see if they can remove the missed payment on your account. **(Protect your credit!)** Then make the payment immediately. I've done this twice before (for two different credit cards) and they removed my missed payment both times. But don't assume they will do it for you. There is variation between credit card companies, and customer service reps. It could also have to do with the fact that I had previous history of on-time payments. I can't say that calling and trying to get a missed payment removed will always work for you, but not calling will definitely get you nowhere.

My story

This is the story all about how my cred got screwed-turned upside down, and I'd like to take a minute so sit right there. And I'll tell you how I got it back up when no hope was there.

When I was in college, I got into some serious money, and credit trouble. I couldn't get a credit card from even the most forgiving credit card companies. I'm going to talk about how I went from a raggedy credit score to a respectable one in 18 months.

It all started the year I graduated high school and was getting ready to move for college. (Class of 2007!) At this point I already had a credit card and was managing it properly. I never looked at my credit score but I did not plan on getting a mortgage any time soon, so who cares right? My little sister was turning 13 and was outgrowing her first bed. We decided to go out as a family to find her a shiny new one. Eventually we arrived at City Furniture. City Furniture was epic! It of course had tons of furniture: chairs, recliners, huge TVs, free cookies, and cushy beds and couches to nap on. We were looking at beds and I was shocked when I saw the prices. $500?! $700?! $850?!!! All I did was smirk. There's no way my frugal mom would buy a bed for this much money. Later my sister found "the bed of her dreams." It had pink sheets, a shiny pink bed skirt, a white chamfered pillar at each corner, and a vail-like sheet flowing from the canopy. I looked at the price tag and almost died. $1,100?! WTH?! I couldn't believe the audacity of my little sister, and I was even more shocked at the pleasant smile on my mother's face. My mom couldn't spend $300 on an Xbox 360 for me, but now she ready to drop $1,100 on my little sister's bed? I was hot. But it wasn't over. Later I found that the reason my mom brought me, wasn't so I could help them find the perfect bed, it was so she could open a

City Furniture credit card IN MY NAME! Now I'm fuming! I couldn't believe it. The secrecy, the audacity, the betrayal. But in the end, I had to do it. Between the big moon-sized crocodile tears in my little sister's eyes, and my mom giving me the death stare, I did it. She is my one and only sister after all. Anyway, my credit was good enough to get me my 2nd credit card, so we came home with the canopy bed.

Within the first semester of my college life, my mom made all the payments on time, month after month until it was paid off. I destroyed that card because I didn't plan on using it ever again. In the meantime, I started getting credit card approval letters left and right. I knew better; I never opened any of them. But then Infinity Ward dropped one of the hottest, most revolutionary video games of all time. Call Of Duty 4: Modern Warfare. This game had it all:

great guns, precise game mechanics, and the online play was just insane! After playing at my friends' dorm rooms every night, till 2 in the morning, they started getting annoyed with me. They'd say things like, "When are you going to get your own Xbox?" Or "hey man, you play it more than me, and I live here." Or "get out of my fridge". I was an addict. So, what could I do? I destroyed my City Furniture card after my mom paid off the bed, and my first credit card only had a limit of $300, so with a twitch in my neck, and sleep deprived blood-shot eyes, I applied for a new credit card. My credit score was good enough to get me approved for $3,000. It was the worst financial decision I ever made. TO BE CONTINUED...

2. Credit Utilization ratio

Credit Utilization Ratio, calculated by FICO, is worth 30% of your credit score.

A credit limit is the maximum amount a credit card company allows a customer to utilize on a specific card. For example, let's say you have a credit card with a credit limit of $1,000. If you charge $400 on clothes #treatyoself it would look like this.

$$Credit\ Utilization\ Ratio = \frac{400}{1000} = 40\%$$

The lower your ratio, the higher your score can be. The industry standard, "satisfactory ratio" is less than 30% utilization. It's not wise to carry a balance on a credit card, especially if that charge pushes the utilization ratio over 30%--for any one card. Sometimes credit cards need to be used for emergencies, which is understandable, but it's important to pay off any large charges as soon as possible. To maximize your score, you must keep your utilization ratio low.

The chart below shows credit utilization ratios compared to a GPA.

Ratio	GPA
5%-9%	4.0 (A)
10%-15%	3.5 (B)
16%-29%	3.0 (C)
30%-50%	2.0 (D)
51%-89%	1.0 (F)
90%-100%	0.0 (S) *S is for STOP*

In case you didn't notice, the top row of the table (4.0 GPA) does not include 0%-4%. The reason is because creditors like to see their customers use at least 5% of their credit limit. So, it's pretty much a game of cat and mouse. They want to see you use your money responsibly but at the same time, they don't want you to use too much money because that increases the risk of you missing payments. *All these games!*

If it's difficult to keep your ratio less than 30% (a lil too much Amazon huh?), you need to create a budget, stop using that credit card, and or explore an increase in your credit limit.

Some credit card issuers will raise your limit automatically after 6 months of on-time payments; it is a feature on some credit cards. If your limit doesn't increase after 6 months, you should call your creditor and ask if you're eligible for a credit limit increase. **NOTE:** The act of submitting a request for a limit increase will not affect your credit score.

It's not recommended to submit a request more than once every six months, for the same institution. This could trigger them to think that you're in financial trouble and need money fast.

Having your credit limit increased will reduce your utilization ratio so this is a rare "low risk—high reward" situation. But be careful. Remember, a credit card should be primarily used as a **tool** to build your credit history. If you do increase your credit limit, remember that it is a strategy to lower your credit utilization ratio, not an excuse to buy more stuff and get into more debt.

3. Length of Credit History

The average length of your credit accounts, which is worth 15% of your credit score, is just an average of the length of time that all of your credit accounts have been open. Early in your credit life, closing your first or second credit card significantly impacts your length of credit history—this could even lower your credit score.

For example,

Credit Card #1- 5 years old, $500 limit

Credit Card #2- 3 years old, $800 limit

Total Credit Limit= 500+800 = $1300

Length of Credit History =

$$\frac{3yrs + 5yrs}{2 \ credit \ cards} = 4 \ years$$

As you grow in your career, you'll begin to make more money, and spend more money. You'll need a card with a higher limit, but you don't want to have too many credit cards. So you close your first card to open a new credit card with a higher limit of $1,500. Your credit limit rose from $1,300 to $2,300.

Great, right? Not necessarily. There are a couple of things to remember. Because you closed an account before opening a new one, your total credit limit dropped before it went up. As a result your utilization ratio temporarily went up. And because you closed your **oldest** account, your "average length of credit" went from 4 years to 1.5 years! Ouch! That's a big loss in credit history! That's no bueno for your credit score. Trading up to a bigger card may not make your score jump as much as you had hoped if you don't strategize. Time is valuable, use it to your advantage. It's helpful to maintain long standing credit.

The best move here is to ask for a credit limit increase on your $500 card, and see if the increase is sufficient for your purchasing needs. If the increase isn't enough, then open another credit card account. Once you have history with a new card (1-2 years), pay off the first card and close the account. You will lose on average length of accounts, but it won't be as significant a hit as closing the card before you open your new one. Your credit limit increase should be able to over shadow this smaller history loss, since utilization ratio has twice as much impact on your score as history length.

4. New Credit and Credit Inquiries

Another factor is new credit and credit inquiries. It is worth 10%. Whenever you are opening a new credit account (i.e. credit card, loan, etc...) the institution administers a hard inquiry or "hit" on your credit. This is when they officially validate your credit (report and score) to qualify and approve you for more credit. What's stupid about it, is that it brings down your credit score! Like what the freak bro?! So, if I'm trying to increase my credit score by decreasing my utilization ratio, I'll need to take a hit on my credit which will bring my credit score down first? Perfect! A hit on your credit could make your credit score drop anywhere between 1-5 points, so you need to avoid them as much as possible.

Even those new to credit, should avoid opening too many credit cards at the same time. Banks have individuals hired specifically to analyze your tendencies, and calculate the risk in increasing or giving you credit. If you apply for 6 credit cards at once, that type of behavior could be interpreted as "you are in financial trouble and need immediate access to a lot of money, and therefore a risky candidate."

I had a horrible experience with this the first time I bought a vehicle through a dealership after college. Those fools hit my credit 8 times trying to find a lender to approve my mediocre credit score. If you think there's even a tiny chance someone is going to hit your credit, and you didn't know they were going to, you need to stop and question them immediately! Your credit is very important and should be protected at all costs! These inquiries stay on your credit report for 24 months (2 years) so you should really think about that before applying for a bunch of cards!

5. Number of credit account types

The number of credit types you have is also worth 10% of your credit score. Paying different types of debt (i.e. credit cards, mortgages, student loans, etc...) indicates that you can take on any and all forms of financial responsibility. One thing to keep in mind is that it may not be possible to have a great score in this area early in your credit journey. You may not get a nice score until you start a mortgage or auto loan.

So there are all of the credit factors. Recognize that if your score is going down—or isn't going up—it's for one of the reasons we just discussed. So you at least have somewhere to start to figure out why your score isn't where you think it should be.

My story, continued...

This was my first time with this much freedom and this much money so I went ham! A college student with a $3,000 credit limit is bad news if they don't know how to use it. I didn't have a job or that many bills and I somehow racked up over $2500 of debt buying an Xbox 360, 2 controllers, a Samsung flat screen, several games, rock band instruments, new clothes and anything else I wanted.

I started making payments on the card with my financial aid money. I was a cheapskate so I was making only the minimum payments. I transferred to a bigger university because I wanted more opportunity (shout out to UCF!). Over the next 2-3 years it felt like that credit card debt barely moved. A couple months later, the rack and pinion broke on my Chevy Impala. I had to drop close to $900 to fix it. I was pissed. I used my financial aid money to pay it because my credit card balance was still too high. At this point, I had to get a job. I was headed down an ugly path.

I was using my financial aid to pay my rent, but because I used some of it to pay for the car repairs, the funds ran out early. Luckily, with the money from my little job, I had enough to make my minimum payment on the credit card and was still able to pay rent. Later, my mom wasn't doing so well, and my grades were falling because of it. I really needed more time to dedicate to studying so I stopped working. I began to fall back on rent payments since my financial aid ran out. So eventually I sold my car to make a big dent in my rent debt so I wouldn't get kicked out.

Throughout this last 7-8 months of college, I didn't make one credit card payment because paying for rent was priority. That Capital One credit card had a $3,000 limit, and it eventually blew into a $4,000 debt after interest and fees. I was reported to collections, law offices were calling me left and right. My credit score dropped below 600. I tried to open another credit card several times but I wasn't approved. I didn't know about hard inquiries so I probably got 10-12 in that one month of trying to get another credit card. I eventually had to get food stamps. Everything bad was hitting me all at once. I owed money on my credit card, I owed money for my apartment, my car was gone, my pride wouldn't let me ask for my parents help, plus my mom needed to use her own money for her meds. I was at rock bottom. The last place I applied for a credit card told me my credit score was around 550.

TO BE CONTINUED...

Chapter 4: Applying for a Credit Card

Research, research, research. There are tons of credit cards out there. Don't be a schmuck—like I was—and apply for credit cards because you need the money. Wait until you're in a financially stable place and can make responsible choices. Are you a frequent flyer? Are you planning to use it for gas and food? Emergencies? Every person has different habits. It is your responsibility to research the best possible card for your situation. Credit cards are starting to go crazy with rewards and cashback programs. I have a capital one card and it gives me 1.5% cash back on anything I buy. EVERYTHING. I used the card for 3 months and racked up $20 in cash back rewards. I converted that to Amazon gift cards! Who wouldn't love that?

Secured Credit card (New/Bad credit)

Everything we've covered up to this point has been in regards to an unsecured credit card—that's what traditional credit cards are classified as. If you are new to credit cards or have bad credit consider getting a secured credit card to help learn how to manage a credit card, and increase your score quickly. A secured credit card is one in which the credit limit is established by you. You have to deposit your own money into the account. (ex. $700 deposit = $700 credit limit) Psychologically, we tend to treat things better when we used our hard earned money to get it.

Pros

- Secured cards can report to the major credit bureaus, but make sure yours does. If not, it's useless for building your credit.
- A lot easier to get approved vs traditional credit cards.
- It helps you control your spending habits.
- Your initial deposit poses as a security deposit of sorts to the credit card company. It

will be snatched if you default on your payments. But what this does mean is you will NOT get sent to collections for defaulting on your payments! That is, assuming your balance is less than the deposit. (P.S. interest and late fees are what could cause your balance to be over your deposit/limit amount)

I'm sure you can see why this is an excellent option for those struggling to build their credit. This is one of the few options you have when you have bad credit.

Cons

- You have to make an initial deposit.
- Higher interest rates than unsecured cards.
- More fees. (You will be charged a hefty fee for missing a payment)
- Depending on your situation you could only afford a low limit if you don't have a lot

of money to deposit, which puts you at risk to have a high utilization ratio.

- Your credit limit will not automatically go up after making on-time payments, and you can't ask them to increase it. (unsecured cards do not have this capability most of the time)

This card exists to help you learn to manage your credit so that you will develop good habits. It will prepare you for an unsecured card, aka a Big Boi card.

PRO TIP

After using a secured card for a year you may be able to ask the issuer to convert it into an unsecured card! It's a sweet offer. Not all issuers have it, and it's not available all the time. You will have to call and ask if they have the offer. If not, have them call you when it's available. By converting it, you will keep all the credit history you've accumulated on the card! If you have cards with low limits, try to have those credit limits moved to other cards (or combined). Some issuers can do this if the cards are from the same company.

Chapter 5: Tips and Suggestions

Credit Cards are serious business. Making large purchases on luxury items when you know you can't make the minimum payment is stupid. If you can't afford it, don't get it! DO NOT go into debt trying to keep up with the latest fashion trend, or trying to be fly. If you have to go into debt to get the newest Coach bag, you can't afford it. If you get it and you can't make the payments, you will damage your credit score, and impact your other financial plans in the future. There are people struggling to get back on their feet because of the one time they bought the new Jordan's on credit. You might be cool and look fly but you'll also be going in debt voluntarily. Trust me, once you graduate, real life hits you. The Jordan's you bought to impress Brittany junior year — will be the least of your worries. **Note:** Don't rely on credit cards as your only means to pay your bills or buy luxury items. Don't let it become a crutch. You're setting yourself up to get screwed.

Creditors = High School Girls

Treat credit cards like you should have treated that girl you were trying to date in high school:

   o Don't use your card too much (open too many accounts/ have too high of a balance) that makes it seem like you are dependent on the credit. Creditors will be "turned off" by your desperation and clinginess. Just like Sarah was sophomore year.

   o It's also not a good idea to totally ignore your card all together. The creditors aren't making any money from interest they'd charge you, or transaction fees that they charge the businesses you shop at. Your unused card is also at a higher risk of being targeted for identity theft. So, the creditors may close your account for nonuse. Just like how Keisha shut it down when you didn't call her last

Summer. Having an account closed on you could bring down your credit score for two reasons.

1. Your length of credit history could go down
2. If you have a balance on other cards your credit utilization ratio will go up.

- The sweet spot is to use the card just enough to keep creditors interested. You consistently charge to the card in small to medium amounts and consistently pay it off. Give it the reasonable level of attention you wish you'd given Keisha.

Tracking Your Credit

Use a credit tracking service if you're worried about identity theft. You can get a free credit report from several different websites like: Annualcreditreport.com, freecreditreport.com, or experian.com. Checking your own credit score will not affect your credit.

Credit Karma is a website that gives valuable information about your credit. The site pulls info straight from Experian and Transunion, two of the three credit bureaus. **Note**: There is some lag between when you do something that affects your credit, and when the CB updates your credit report.

Set It and Forget It

If you put one or two bills on a credit card (i.e. Cell phone bill, Netflix, etc...) and then establish autopay, your credit card limit and score could increase in as little as 6 months!

Here's my personal real-life example:

- Credit card due date – 25th
- Hulu due date – 10th

On Hulu.com I set it up so my credit card pays the Hulu bill every month on the 10th automatically. Then I have the credit card pay that balance off by pulling from my checking account automatically on the 20th. (I like to leave some days in between the day I pay and the due date for processing). You may also be able to pay your credit card balance from your bank's online website.

It's almost as efficient as using a debit card, but you're building credit too. Set it and forget it, all from the convenience of your computer. This keeps cards active, especially those with lower limits, and increase your limit and score.

Become an authorized user

Personally speaking, this strategy had the quickest impact on my credit. It increased my credit score over 15 points in only 3 weeks! Becoming an authorized user on a trusted family or friend's credit card is one of the best weapons in your arsenal. Have the card holder either call the credit card company, or sign up online to apply. The benefits are too good to pass up. You are added to their credit card account and benefit from their credit history! The length of credit history and the credit limit will now be applied to yours. Shortcut! This is a trick that savvy financial parents do for their kids! **Note:** Only use this strategy with a trusted person with a good history paying their credit cards. Their bad habits will impact your credit score too.

Making credit card payments

There are drawbacks to making payments too quickly. There is no extra incentive to pay off your purchases every three days. Creditors want customers that use their cards. Paying it all the way down very quickly will probably not hurt your credit score, but your credit score will not increase if you continue to do this. If you have a credit score over 800, and you don't use your card, your score will go down automatically. The trick is to use the card, let enough time pass for the credit company to see your balance, and then pay the balance before the due date.

Bottom Line

The more tips you know, the easier it will be to succeed. So remember:

- Creditors are like high school girls.
- Track your status, and progress with free credit websites.
- Use the set it and forget it method.
- Become an authorized user on a trusted person's account.
- Do not pay your balances immediately, let the creditors see that you use your card
- A trusted credit card user:
    - Has a credit card with an average balance of 5%-9% of their limit per month.

o   Pays the balance in full, on time, every month over an extended period of time.

If you can manage this with any of your credit cards, you'll be on track to baller status. Creditors will love you.

Chapter 6: Credit Card Debt

Owing someone money can be tough, owing an institution is on a whole 'nother level! It's pretty easy to fall into debt. Americans are in so much debt, specifically, credit card debt. That's why this subject deserves its own chapter.

Getting out of debt gets more and more difficult because interest builds upon itself. It's called compound interest (explained later). Overall, debt is kind of like a student and their GPA.

Say you've been a great student as a freshman and sophomore and built a 3.5 GPA Then you have one bad semester and your GPA drops to 3.25. Guess what? You now have to be almost flawless for the next two years to get back to that 3.5 GPA (The struggle is real!)

Get it in your mind that Debt = Slavery. Even the bible says so! Check Proverbs 22:7 (NIV), "The rich rule over the poor, and the borrower is **slave** to the lender." I haven't heard anything more real and troubling in my life. We know debt is bad, but when it's mentioned in the good book like that, we should probably take it seriously.

As an example, let's say we messed up, and now we have several avenues of debt. We have credit card debt, we have medical bills from little Timmy's surgery, and we still have those annoying student loans. What should we do? Which one should we pay off first? Should we just ignore it? Check out some of these strategies.

Strategies for Paying off Debt

Snowball #1 (lowest balance)

1. Stop using your credit cards! Duh!
2. Identify all your debts.
3. Make minimum payment on all but one.

   (the one with the **lowest balance**)
4. On that low balance debt pay as much

as you can, the more you pay, the faster you'll pay it off. Sacrifice that concert ticket or your "fast food every day" diet, in order to add more money to the payment. Pack a sandwich, block out your inner fatty!

5.   Once you pay off that debt, add that payment amount to the next lowest debt payment. You'll be paying that one off even faster!

6.   When you finally pay off that debt, move the payment amount from the 1st and 2nd debt to pay off your third debt. Now you'll be zooming! You'll have the payment amount from the 1st debt, the 2nd debt, and the 3rd debt. Where all this money come from, bruh?

7.   If you keep your focus you'll be debt free in no time!

As you pay off a debt, that amount is then added to the next debt, which is why it's referred to as a snowball method. The amount of money you add to the next debt grows bigger and bigger! Soon your payments will be so huge, you'll be paying off debt in a few years rather than decades.

Snowball #2 (highest interest rate)

Mathematically speaking, to truly save the most money, you need to pay the debt with the **highest interest rate** first. So this second snowball method is the same as the first but instead of starting with the lowest balance debt you start with the one that has the highest interest rate. This isn't always practical for us normal folk. Normally those debts would take a lot longer to pay off by comparison. As a young grasshopper, you need to build habits, and one of the easiest ways to do that is with baby steps. Doing the lowest balance method you begin to pick up momentum easier. Milestones come quicker and you begin to feel your confidence build just as quickly as your payment amounts. It's an amazing feeling! Using the highest interest rate method will save you money in the long run, but it takes much more discipline. And it won't give you that instant gratification #Millennials.

Other options

If you are really serious about getting rid of your debt, you should consider ALL your options. Keep in mind that in life when you are deciding either to save, invest, or pay off debt, know that paying off debt is one of the guaranteed ways to get return on your investment. These following suggestions are only for people in desperate situations, those who will try anything to get out of debt. Check out these options to supplement your payments.

- You may consider using some money from your emergency savings account.
- Refinance your mortgage, or get an equity loan on something else of value. **Note**: This will be explained further in a future book. If the interest rate would be lower than your current interest rate, it's a viable option.
- Ask family and friends. This is a polarizing suggestion. Many people will tell you to never mix money with friends and family. It's totally understandable. You need

to decide how long it will take you to get out of debt. In my personal opinion, so long as you plan, and create a schedule of payments, it's worth the risk. I'd rather owe money to Uncle Gary than Uncle Sam. Where the government and banks would charge you interest, drop your credit score, and garnish your wages, Uncle Gary would charge you in teaching him how to use "That Face-Gram" thing.

- Use other credit cards with a 0% balance transfer. A balance transfer is when you move the balance from one credit card to another. (Basically, you're paying off one credit card with another) Most of the time, credit cards have a fee for doing this, but there are cards that exist for just this purpose. Say you have a credit card debt of $3,000 with a nasty interest rate. You might consider getting a 0% balance transfer credit card with a lower interest rate. You'll get yourself some extra time to come up with the money, and you'll save on interest. Some of these cards have an introductory offer in which you pay 0% in interest for 12 months or more. With these two features at your disposal, you'll essentially have 12 months to pay off that $3,000 debt without having to worry about accruing interest!

How to deal with the stress of debt

Debt is a part of life. We feel like if we're in debt that means our finances are screwed up, but the reality is, almost everybody is in debt. That's because we've been fed to believe it's normal to be in debt. In a future book, we will explore how to break away from conventional financial knowledge, and join the realm of financial freedom. But you gotta know the rules to beat the game. That's why this book is an important first step.

Personal thoughts

If you feel the thought of having to pay off something huge over 30 years scares or bothers you, consider this: There are certain bills we need to pay **forever** so why aren't we all stressed about those? Sound crazy? Hear me out. Take your car and homeowner's insurance. You cannot pay those off, which means theoretically it can be thought of as a debt that will last your lifetime—in comparison to something like student loans.

For instance, let's say your car insurance for two cars is $250/mo, you are 25 years old, and you drive until you're 70 years old. Check this out:

$$\left(\frac{\$250}{mo}\right) x \ (70 \ yrs - 25 \ yrs) \ x \ 12 \ months/yr = \$135,000$$

That means, for your lifespan, you're shelling out anywhere around $135,000 for car insurance! We don't think about it that way but in reality, that's how much we're paying. So, a student loan debt of let's say $40,000 over 30 years doesn't seem as bad now does it? It's all about perspective. So, try not to get depressed about debt.

Get rid of other expenses

Here's another way to think about it. Let's say you have a student loan payment of $250/mo for 30 years. That means you are now losing an extra $250/mo. But what if you cut cable and go the streaming route? That's an extra $75 more a month. What if you pay off your new phone in about 24 months? That's $25/mo more. Pay off your car? That's $250/mo. What if you find cheaper insurance? That's $50/mo more a month. What about all your raises from work? That's an extra $50-$100/mo. If you add that all together, that's an extra $500/mo. And most of those things can happen within the next 24 months. The point is, don't put yourself in a hole of despair. If you have a large "scary" debt, think about it in terms of a monthly cost. Instead of freaking out, take control by looking at the "less scary" ones to pay off. Pay those off to free up extra money every month to tackle the big beast. I really hope that eases your mind a little bit in regards to debt.

Defaulting (Hardships)

Defaulting is when life takes a dump on you and you become super past due on your payments. (i.e. you miss payments for 6 consecutive months) They will report you to the CB. THIS IS BAD. It's pretty much the worst thing that can happen to you — as far as building your credit goes. Not only does defaulting drop your credit score a lot. It stands out on your credit report like a sore thumb. There are also other negative effects to consider. For example, some credit issuers won't approve you for a credit card or loan until you've cleared up the default. But your life isn't over; there are several things you can do to get out of this situation. We'll talk about them next.

1. Pay off the balance

Obviously. If you have the cash or can get the cash don't waste time, pay it off ASAP! No matter what you do or how long you hold out, the creditors are going to get money one way or another. Paying

74

off the debt ASAP is the quickest way to get out of this proverbial pit.

PRO TIP

Before you make a payment, first negotiate for the default status to be removed from your credit report in exchange for paying off the full balance.

2.   Negotiate to pay less

Some debt collectors are willing to resolve the issue if you make a lump sum payment. Potentially for less than what you owe. The reason you can pay less than you owe is because the bank can write off the loss on their taxes (taxes discussed later). The bank can take the loss directly, by letting you pay them less, but in a lot of cases, the bank will sell your debt to a 3rd party collection agency at a much lower price than what you owed. And then the 3rd party will start calling you trying to get more from you then they paid to the bank. If the bank or a 3rd party elects to have you pay less than you originally owed, you will have to pay taxes on the amount they let you slide. That amount will be added to your taxable income for the year.

3.   File bankruptcy
(CONSULT AN EXPERT)

Depending on how much trouble you're in, you might want to consider filing for bankruptcy. It can make your payments more affordable, or it may forgive your debt all together. But this isn't some free pass; it stays on your credit report for 7 - 10 years! So you will have a difficult time getting approved for new credit cards or loans for the next 7 - 10 years. Do not consider this option unless you are really in a bad place financially, you've exhausted all your options, and you've spoken to a couple experts about it.

4.   Do nothing.

Some people think "maybe if I just ignore them, the debt will go away" or "they'll stop asking me for it". This is a dangerous mindset. You can decide to "do nothing". Just know the creditor will still pursue you for the debt and throw all sorts of shade on your credit report. As mentioned before, they will "sell" the rights to collect your debt to someone else. Then you will start receiving phone calls from other institutions trying to collect the debt. "Hi, this is an attempt to collect a debt". UGGHHH! That was one of the scariest moments in my life. I was scared to pick up the phone if I didn't know the number – for fear of getting a debt collector on the line.

Lastly, if you don't resolve the debt, they could **SUE YOU** and get the government involved. Ouch! If they win the case, they may be able to garnish (legally take) your wages! That means part of your hard-earned paycheck will go to the creditors to pay off the debt. Nasty stuff.

PRO TIP

If you're getting a bunch of calls from third-party debt collectors, you can make them stop by mailing them a "**cease and desist**" letter. Make sure you send the letter via **certified mail**. (It makes the mailman ask for a signature--from the creditor--to prove that it was received) Don't forget to save a copy of the letter for your records. **NOTE:** You **cannot** use the cease and desist letter with the original creditor. It only works for third-party debt collectors. For the sake of space, a sample cease and desist letter can be found in the free workbook.

Well that's the basics of building your credit. Now that you know the basics, you can put yourself in the right position to stay out of debt.

In summary

- Don't put anything on credit without having a firm plan of how you will budget to pay it off.

- Make sure to never miss a payment for bills that affect your credit, **no matter what**. Shift the other bills around if you must.

- Set up a "set it and forget it" system for credit cards using auto-pay features.

- Always seek lower interest rates when you're credit score goes up.

- Get out of debt ASAP. Interest will eat away at your payments if you don't.

- It's okay that you don't know everything right away. Instead of trying to memorize it use this book as a reference.

- **PROTECT YOUR CREDIT BY ANY MEANS NECESSARY.**

Next, we're hitting up Credit's annoying uncle, Taxes. But before that, let's finish the story.

My story, continued...

Well this was senior year and I decided, I just needed to get out of this mess. I met my future wife and she helped me buck up. It's like I got a 2nd wind. My mom was recovered, I got another job, and started paying off my rent debt. I had one month left of school and I didn't have enough money to pay for that last month of rent. I had to sell my video game collection, and TV to pay off the last bit of rent I owed. I paid the rent debt first because the school wouldn't give me my degree if I had a debt owed to the housing department. So, I paid it off, and my future wife and I walked across the stage together—one behind the other. I followed her across the stage that day but little did I know I would follow her across the country. After we graduated, my wife moved to Michigan for work. Knowing the whole automotive industry was there, I eventually moved there as a *cough cough* career move. When I moved, I decided I wanted a fresh start, it was time to take care of that credit card debt. I called the law office that kept harassing me, and I created a payment plan. Over the next 6 months, I lived like a bum. After paying bills, and buying groceries, the rest of my check went straight to my credit card debt. After paying it off, my credit score rose to about 600-ish. Not great, but not too shabby for me. Next, I took a chance, and applied for a secured credit card and got one! Capital one again. This time I was diligent about managing my debt. It was so hard to pay off my last credit card; I wasn't about to let that happen again. Not only did I make all my payments on-time, but I called a Capital one debt specialist and had them remove the old delinquency from my credit report. In the next

3 months, my credit score rose to 640. Then I started paying off my whole balance every month, and my credit score rose to 665! I couldn't believe it. In the span of about 18 months my credit score jumped over 100 points. It's crazy how fast it starts to move when you have your crap together.

I'll never forget. At my lowest point, I had a ton of hard inquiries, I defaulted on my credit card, and was sent to collections, couldn't pay my rent and had to get on food stamps. But after a fresh start, I paid off my debt, removed my delinquency notice, and made it to a respectable credit score. I remember when I started getting credit card offers in the mail again, I was thinking to myself, "I'm back!".

Truth is, it's possible to make it back from the brink. I'm living proof. I'm not anyone special. If I can do it, so can you. You can get out of debt. You can turn your life around. You just need to focus, and stop buying frappuccinos, and that fricken avocado toast.

Chapter 7: Taxes

We get taxed a bunch of different ways, for a bunch of different reasons. Some include: income tax, sales tax, property tax, and capital gains tax. Since this is a beginner's book, we'll only go over what you came here for, and that is income tax.

As a base, understand that taxes are fees that individuals or corporations must pay to a government entity (i.e. local, national, etc...). It's used to finance government activities or projects. It is the main source of government funds and is tracked and enforced by the schmucks at the IRS (Internal Revenue Service). The funds go to several different things including: social security, medicare, national defense, healthcare, veteran benefits, immigration, law enforcement, response to natural disasters, and the list goes on and on.

The goal of this chapter is to help you get an understanding of the following things:

- How does the government calculate my taxes?
- How to calculate my own taxes
- How to minimize my tax liability? (How much I owe)
- What forms do I need?
- Where to have my taxes done

Quick definitions

Tax return: a form that consumers fill out that tells the IRS how much money in taxes they paid in the past year, how much tax they still owe, or how much they overpaid.

Tax refund: a reimbursement given to a filer when what they owed was less than the taxes they paid.

A **W4** and **W9** are forms given to you from your employer for you to fill out. It's used to determine how much state and federal income tax to withhold (to save) from your paycheck throughout the year. Basically, they're asking, "how much tax will you need to pay at the end of the year" and withholding that amount. **W4** is for employees. **W9** is for independent contractors. Employees have their tax-withheld by their employer to pay tax on their behalf, independent contractors do not. **Note**: In an effort to save space, W-4 and W-9 forms will be linked in the free workbook.

What is a tax exemption/allowance?

A circumstance that reduces your tax liability (the amount you owe). Basically, it works like this. On your **W4/W9**, you can add one exemption per household person. (i.e. each parent and each dependent) So for example, if you are single, and you worked during the year, you can claim one personal tax exemption yourself. If you are married with no kids and file a joint tax return, both you and your spouse each get an exemption. **Note:** Exemptions reduce your taxable income just like a deduction does, but it has fewer rules in comparison to a deduction.

You can claim any number of allowances which includes up to (you + your dependents) on each **W4**, depending how much or how little taxes you want taken out of your paycheck. For example, if you're married with no kids you can both file zero exemptions and more money will be taken out of your check—which will increase the likelihood of receiving a tax refund. On the other hand, if you want or need a bigger paycheck, you can both file with one exemption. Less money will be taken out of your check, but it increases the likelihood of you having little to no tax refund.

Summary of exemptions (subject to change)

This is the type of information that you shouldn't try to remember. Just wait until the time comes to evaluate your situation and select the correct filing.

Especially with the frequency at which tax policies change.

Single with no kids

- Claiming Zero: If you claim zero, the maximum amount in tax is withheld from your paycheck. This means you're more likely receive a refund when filing your taxes.

- Claiming One: If you are single, have no kids and have one job, if you claim one a smaller amount is withheld from your paycheck for taxes than when claiming zero. You're still likely to receive a refund when filing your taxes, but it may be smaller — because you already got that money throughout the year in the form of bigger pay checks.

- Claiming Two: If you are single and work more than one job, you can claim two at one job and zero at the other, or claim one at each job.

Married with no kids (Filing jointly)

- Claiming Zero: If you have a combined income that falls within the 28% or higher tax brackets (explained later), claim zero and you will owe less money during tax time and may get a tax refund.

- Claiming One: If your combined income falls below the 28% tax bracket and you both work, you could each claim one, you could break even or get a small refund back when filing.

- Claiming Two. If only one of you work and your income falls below the 28% tax bracket, you can claim two.

Married with one or more kids

- Claiming One: If both spouses work, it's beneficial for each of you to claim one. This way you will probably break even come tax season

- Claiming Two: If only one spouse works, the working spouse can claim two and will probably come close to breaking even when filing taxes.
- For each additional child or dependent, just add one to the number of allowances based on the example above.

Note: If someone claims you as a dependent, when they fill out their **W4/W9**, your allowances on your W4/W9 should be zero.

The bottom line is, the more allowances you claim, the smaller the amount of taxes your employer will withhold. If too little is withheld, (also called under-withholding) you could end up with a large tax bill after completing your tax return. This section can be a little tricky or confusing. So definitely ask a lot of questions the first few times when you file your taxes.

When should you update your W4/W9?

- Marriage
- Divorce
- New child
- A second job
- Purchase of a new home
- Death of a spouse or Dependent
- Dependent becoming independent
- Any other big life change that really affects your income

The W-2 (employee)

The W2 is a document that has all the important information such as the money you earned, and the taxes you paid all year long. You need it to properly fill out your tax return. Your employer is supposed to send it to you by Jan 31st. If they don't, ask for it ASAP. Ain't nobody got time for that. We will link it in the free workbook.

The 1099 (Independent contractor)

The 1099 is a form that works the same as a W2 but for an independent contractor. If you are an independent contractor (also called "a 1099") your employer does not withhold your taxes, so you will be responsible to pay taxes on all the money you earned throughout the year. That means you must pay your taxes all on your own. You will most likely owe money at the end of the year to the IRS unless you have expenses/right offs. A sample can be found in the free workbook.

My story continued...

After graduation, I got a quick job with a large chemical company in Michigan. They didn't have any entry-level engineering positions at the time, so I worked for them as a contractor. I decided even though I'm not working in the capacity that I want, I can at least start networking to get my foot in the door. And that's exactly what I did. For 6 months I spoke with directors, supervisors, and other employees during their lunch breaks and through email. I emailed them my resume and someone responded with an offer to interview me. I was super excited; it was pretty much the perfect job for me coming out of school. I thought the stars were aligning. But then it happened.

A couple days after I accepted the interview, the hiring manager told me my interview was "rejected" because of some corporate policy. WTH? It said you cannot work for this company as an employee until you leave your contractor position and let one-year pass. It's called a non-compete clause. WWTTTTHHHH? I was HOT!! My hiring manager did not point this out when I was signing the contract, but I guess it's not their job. Their job is to get people to sign the contract; my job is to read the terms and condition thoroughly, and of course I didn't. So, to advance my career I decided I was going to quit the job. When I told a friend I was thinking about leaving, they told me to make sure that I had enough to pay my taxes. I had no idea what they were talking about.

At the time, I didn't know that as a 1099 contractor, I was paid every dime for all the hours I worked. Nothing from my paychecks was saved for taxes. So, I should've been saving my income to pay taxes at the end of the year— which I obviously hadn't been. **Note**: If you have your stuff together you can pay quarterly instead of at the end of the year.

What made it worse is the fact that I had a desk job, so I had nothing to write off as an expense. As a contractor, when you do your taxes you can write-off work-related expenses which will decrease your tax liability. Some examples are gas—if you're a driver, clothes for work, and all other supplies or services that you must buy on your own, to do your job. I didn't know anything about this contractor stuff, so I had to keep working just to be able to pay for the nice $6,000 tax bill in April. Just my luck. So, again I lived frugally for another 6 months to afford the tax payment, and save for my upcoming wedding and honeymoon. This was one of the most stressful times of my life; I'm so thankful my wife was there to support me.

I made the tax payment, we went on a great honeymoon cruise, and I quit my contractor job. Lesson learned. Contractor roles are fine but, you must do your due diligence to verify you have all the information to succeed. What can you list as expenses, what will my tax bill be? Can I pay it early, etc... If you play your cards right, you can walk away paying little to no tax at all.

Deductions

Deductions or deductibles are expenses that you've made throughout the year that can be written off to lower your taxable income and therefore your tax liability. If you made $50,000 in a year and your total itemized deductible amount is $10,000 then your taxable income drops to $40,000. ($50,000 – $10,000 = $40,000) Policies, rules and regulations do change per state; so please refer to your state's website for the specifics for your area.

Standard Deduction vs Itemizing Deductions

Standard deduction is the flat rate deduction that is given automatically to everyone when filing taxes. For example, in 2016, if you were single (or married filing separately), the standard deduction amount was $6,300. You also have the choice to add up all your deductions (and applicable expenses) to see if you paid more—throughout the year—than the standard deductions. Filing this way is called itemizing your deductions. (Explained later) It's done by filling out a schedule A form.

It's a simple numbers game. If you add up all your itemized deductions and their sum is less than the standard deduction, then your tax liability will be lower if you file with the standard deduction.

Itemized Deductions

The four most common itemized deductions are: Taxes, Interest, Contributions, and Medical Expenses.

Taxes

- Taxes that you pay on your property.
- Taxes that you pay on your vehicles/boat.

- Taxes that you pay on state income tax.

- Taxes that you pay on your consumer goods (sales tax).

Interest

- Mortgage interest.
- Private Mortgage interest (PMI).
- Student loan interest.

Contributions

- Cash donations to charities or religious organizations. (i.e. tithe and offering)
  - Keep track of giving via check or debit card if possible.
- Non-cash donations.
  - Furniture, Appliances, A vehicle, etc...
  - If contributions are above $500 you'll need a written itemization of what you donated.
    - Date of donation
    - Organization you donated to
    - The items that were donated
    - The value of those items

- How you determine those values

Medical Expenses

- Including: co-pays, dental expenses, eye-wear expenses
- Medical miles - 2.5 cents per miles
- Deduct amount that exceeds 10% of your income

How does the government come up with how much tax we should pay?

First, we need to understand tax brackets. The United States uses a progressive tax system, which means different portions of your income are taxed at different rates. You pay a higher overall tax rate if you have a higher taxable income. Tax brackets are just an illustration of this system and show how much you must pay at different income levels. **Note:**

Tax brackets and rates normally change every year so make sure you are using tables for the correct year when filing.

Tax brackets show you the tax rate you will pay on each portion of your income. There is a threshold for each tax level. For example, if you are single, the lowest tax rate of 10% is applied to the first $8,350. The next chunk of your income is then taxed at 15%, then it goes, 25%, 28%, 33%, 35%, and finally 39.6%.

Example:

Let's use the tax bracket numbers for 2009.

Level 1 10% - $8,350

Level 2 15% - $33,950

Level 3 25% - $82,250

Level 4 28% - $171,550

Level 5 33% - $171,551+

Scenario A

- Say you made $100,000 last year.

Scenario B

- Say you made $100,000 last year.
- And you paid $10,000 in mortgage interest. (deductible)

Scenario A

- For **level 1** the first $8,350 of your income gets taxes at 10% ($835).
- For **level 2** the income between $8,351 up to $33,950 is taxed at 15%.
    - The amount taxed in level 2 is the difference between level 2 and level 1 (L2-L1).
    - So L2-L1 = $33,950 - $8,350 = $25,600.
    - So, $256,00 * 15% = $3,840.

- The amount of money in level 3 that will be taxed at 25% is L3-L2 or $82,950-$33,950 = $48,300.
  - So, $48,300 * 25% = $12,075.
- Lastly, for level 4 you'll need to subtract your total income minus level 3 to get level 4.
  - So, $100,000 - $82,250 = $17,750.
  - Then $17,750 * 28% = $4,970.

Sum it all up all levels (L1+L2+L3+L4+L5 = The tax you owe)

- $835 + $3840 + $12075 + $4970= $21,720.

So, you will have owed $21,720 in taxes.

Scenario B

Everything through level 3 is identical to scenario A.

So L1 + L2 + L3 = $835 + $3840 + $12075.

- For level 4 you'll need to subtract your total income minus level 3.
- So, $100,000 - $82,250 = $17,750.

- Because of your **deduction** you'll then go $17,750 - **$10,000** = $7,750.
- So, in **level 4** you'll only get taxed 28% on $7,750 as opposed to $17,750.
  - $7,750 * 28% = $2,170.

Sum up all levels, (L1+L2+L3+L4) = The tax you owe.

- $835 + $3,840 + $12,075 + $2,170 = $18,920.

The difference between scenario A and B is: $21,720 - $18,920 = $2,800 in savings

When you're done filing, your tax preparer (or the software you're using), will tell you how much your refund will be – if any. Then you'll have to pay for the service, and any other taxes. (property, city, state if applicable)

Other questions & answers about taxes

Ways to file

- Online at home
  - o Turbotax.com (Paid software)
  - o Irs.gov (They provide free software for anyone up to $58,000/yr)

- Paid tax services - H&R block, Liberty Tax
  - o More expensive
  - o Less headache
  - o They will help you if you get audited
  - o You know for sure it's filed correctly, peace of mind

How much does it cost?

According to cbsnews.com the average fee at the national tax service firms H&R Block and Liberty

Tax Service is $147 per return and $191 per return, respectively.

- Filing your tax return
  - Choose the right form
    - **1040ez, 1040A,** and **1040**
    - Plug in your personal info, included on your W2/1099 and the software will tell you which form you'll need to fill out.
- Fill out a schedule A(itemize) if applicable.
- Pay your taxes by April 15th
  - If you can't file your taxes by that date, you'll need to fill out a **4868** form. This form gives you a 6-month extension.

Audit

- A tax audit is an examination of your tax return by the IRS. It's to verify that your income and deductions are accurate.

- The IRS audits files that have red flags, and they also audit files at random.

Tax refund dates are based on when the IRS accepts the tax return, so they vary. Therefore, the actual tax refund date could be 20 days after the IRS tax return was accepted, or as early as a week—if you use the direct deposit method.

What to do with the refund?

- Saving
- Pay off debt
- Vacation
- Invest

Summary

- Keep **W4/W9** current, update if there are major changes in your life
- Collect all **W2s** and **1099** forms
- Track and keep all expenses

- Mortgage interest paid on residence
- Mortgage interest paid on investment property
- Expense on major home repairs
- Rental income
- Student loan interest payments
- Miles driven (1099)
- Business expenses (1099)

- File your tax return

  1. If you can't file by April 15th, file for an extension (**4868 form**)

- Wait for a refund to drop!

Conclusion

Well you've made it to the end. Congratulations! I hope this has been informative or even eye-opening. A lot of the things in this book were learned the hard way. But realize I struggled and failed so you don't have to. Don't repeat the same mistakes I made. Learn from them, and share them with others.

Don't let this distract you from the fact that...

This is only book #1 of the My Money Cheat Sheet series. Don't get on your high horse just yet. There is still more to learn before you are fully equipped. Things like Mortgages, Auto loans, Student loans, Work Benefits, and Investing to say a few. You still have much to learn young grasshopper.

One. More. Thing.

Listen, if you made it this far in the book, That's awesome! That means you found value in it, and you may have even learned a thing or two. If that's true I'd really appreciate if you could left a review on Amazon. I want others to know that there's someone out there looking out for them.

References

1. Paying yourself first.
http://www.investopedia.com/terms/p/payyourselffirst.asp
2. 50/30/20 rule.
https://www.thebalance.com/the-50-30-20-rule-of-thumb-453922
3. Credit score vs credit report.
https://www.wellsfargo.com/financial-education/basic-finances/build-the-future/cash-credit/credit-score-report/
4. Credit Bureau.
http://www.investopedia.com/terms/c/creditbureau.asp
5. What affects your credit.
http://budgeting.thenest.com/bills-affect-credit-score-25808.html
6. Interest rate and compound interest.
http://www.debthelp.com/kc/177-do-interest-rates-work.html

7. Effective interest rate.

https://www.inc.com/encyclopedia/annual-percentage-rate-apr.html

8. Calculating interest rates.

https://www.thebalance.com/average-daily-balance-finance-charge-calculation-960236

9. Ask for better interest rate.

http://www.creditcards.com/credit-card-news/script-negotiate- better-credit-card-deal-1267.php

10. Credit ranges.

https://www.credit.com/credit-scores/what-is-a-good-credit-score/

http://www.experian.com/blogs/ask-experian/credit-education/score-basics/what-is-a-good-credit-score/

11. Credit factors.

https://www.wellsfargo.com/financial-education/basic-finances/financial-challenges/repair-credit/affect-credit-score/

12. Applying for a credit card.

https://www.nerdwallet.com/blog/credit-cards/apply-for-a-credit-card/

13. Secured credit card.

http://www.bankrate.com/finance/credit-cards/10-questions-before-getting-a-secured-credit-card-1.aspx

14. How to have your limit increased.

http://www.cardrates.com/advice/how-to-increase-your-credit-limit/

15. Authorized user.

https://www.nerdwallet.com/blog/finance/authorized-user-credit-score/

16. Balance transfer credit card.

http://www.creditcards.com/credit-card-news/help/9-things-you-should-know-about-balance-transfers-6000.php

17. Defaulting on a loan.

https://smartasset.com/mortgage/what-really-happens-if-you-default-on-a-mortgage

18. Tax refund.

https://turbotax.intuit.com/tax-tools/tax-tips/General-Tax-Tips/Do-The-Math--Understanding-Your-Tax-Refund/INF26173.html

19. Expense and deductions.

https://turbotax.intuit.com/tax-tools/tax-tips/Family/Tax-Exemptions-and-Deductions-for-Families/INF12053.html

20. W2 and W4.

https://quickbooks.intuit.com/r/hr-laws-and-regulation/differences-between-irs-forms-w-2-and-w-4/

21. W2 vs 1099.

https://www.learnvest.com/knowledge-center/the-difference- between-a-1099-and-a-w-2/

22. Standard vs Itemized deductions.

https://www.hrblock.com/get-answers/taxes/adjustments-and-deductions/standard-vs-itemized-deductions-10729

23. 2009 Tax charts.

http://www.bankrate.com/finance/money-guides/2009-tax-bracket-rates.aspx

24. How much do you pay a tax preparer?

http://www.cbsnews.com/news/how-much-do-you-pay-for-tax-prep/

25. How long until I get my tax refund?

https://www.efile.com/tax-refund/where-is-my-refund/

About the author

Sam Woke is the embodiment of all millennials. He loves superhero movies, the latest tech, he's surfs social media while he's surfing social media, and he hates debt. He's been through some tough times but they've made him stronger and wiser. If you'd like to connect, you can follow him on the **Sam Woke** Facebook page.

62708891R00076

Made in the USA
Middletown, DE
23 August 2019